GHOSTS
SPIRITS
AND
SPECTRES
OF
SCOTLAND

By Francis Thompson

Illustrated by
John Mackay

INTRODUCTION

THE court case started on a ghost's evidence . . . how an islander returned from the grave to save his wife from a life of poverty . . . when a woman's superhuman power helped locate a missing farmer's body . . . why the cutlery handles soaked in blood gave a murder victim revenge over his killer . . . eerie shadows that foretold of the disastrous defeat on Culloden Field.

These are just a few of the stories explored by Francis Thompson in the pages of Ghosts, Spirits and Spectres of Scotland.

This condensed edited facsimile of the original Impulse edition also tells of the grim murder secret in a Glasgow bathroom, the maid who was followed by an eerie knocking sound no matter where she went, a skeleton hand in Glamis Castle, a floating head which terrorised Dundee hotel guests, the dead wife who saved a fishing boat crew from a watery grave and the three spirits who went a-haunting because they didn't like their burial place.

Find out too about the young man rescued from a desert island by a stranger in return for giving up his children and half his wife, the remarkable cloak of darkness which made its wearer invisible because of the pity of the living for the bones of the dead, mysterious balls of fire on lochs, corpse candle omens which preceded funeral routes, battles fought by phantom warriors before and after the actual event, the man hanged before a crowd of seven thousand because of a dream, and many more unusual tales.

Front cover illustration: A young woman's grim discovery at Culloden — see the story in Strange Happenings chapter.

Back cover: The decaying floating head comes towards her! See the full story in Tales of Horror chapter.

Ghosts Spirits and Spectres of Scotland, a condensed edited reprint of the Impulse 1973 original, was published in 1984 by Lang Syne Publishers Ltd., Newtongrange, Midlothian, and printed by Waterside Printers, Old School, Blanefield, Stirlingshire.

The illustrations by John Mackay are published here for the first time.

© LANG SYNE PUBLISHERS LTD. 1984. REPUBLISHED BY ARRANGEMENT WITH FRANCIS THOMPSON.

ISBN No. 0 946264 99 6

GHOSTS OF THE DEAD

THE stories about ghosts of the dead are as numerous and as varied as one might expect. Many hauntings seem to have been made with a particular purpose: to put right some wrong; to inform the living of something left undone; to warn of impending disaster; to exact some kind of revenge. The following selection indicates the wide variety of ghost 'types' and the bases of their haunting activities.

The wife of a fisherman in Sleat, Skye, had recently been made a widow and was in no little distress as her husband had passed on without leaving any indication as to whether or not he had left any money which she could use to tide her over the early days of her misfortune. One night, while a storm raged outside the thick walls of her cottage, she saw her husband's ghost enter the room, clad in dripping oilskins. As she watched, quite unable to utter a word, the apparition crossed the floor of the room, in the direction of the fireplace. There the figure paused. Then, with a slow and deliberate movement, he made as if to remove a brick. He turned and, with a final gesture of farewell, he disappeared from her sight. After she had recovered from her initial shock, a strong sense of curiosity made her examine the fireplace carefully. Surely, she found a loose brick which she removed to find,

He moves a fireplace brick

in the exposed cavity, a considerable sum of money: her husband's savings of which she had known absolutely nothing. He had in fact returned from the unknown to reveal them to her.

The summer of 1873 saw a young man named Ranold, from South Uist, who was a widower, his dearly loved wife having died a few months previously. In an effort to forget his misfortune, he engaged himself as a hired man with the skipper of a fishing boat belonging to Fraserburgh. In time, the boat was fishing on a good bank some sixty miles to seaward from that town. About the end of the fishing season, while the boat was 'riding at its drift,' in the water of the bank, Ranold found himself taking his turn to watch on deck, while the rest of the crew turned in to take a well-earned rest and nap till daybreak. He relates:

'My duty on deck was to keep a strict lookout that our nets would not be tampered with, and that our lantern burned properly, so as to warn passing vessels of the boat's position, and thus prevent a collision with her. The night in question was pretty dark, and a fresh breeze of wind was blowing. After the crew went to their berths, all being quiet, I sat down with my back to the main-mast (for it had not been lowered that night, as was customary, as there were no signs of any considerable wind springing up before morning), lighted my pipe, and vacantly looked over the vast waste of water, as far as my eyes could penetrate through the darkness. I did not occupy this position for long (I confess it with shame) when I imperceptibly fell asleep.

'As to how long I slept I cannot say, but while sleeping I dreamed that my deceased wife came to me and in her usual sweet and pleasant manner, in an audible voice, said: " Ranold, Ranold, my dear Ranold! Get up quickly and kindle your light. If you do not do so immediately, you will be all lost! " She spoke with such authority and serious- ness that I instantly awoke, and, on looking around me, I saw a large ship bearing swiftly down upon our boat. I at once lighted a candle (for the light of our lantern had somehow been extinguished) and exhibited it. Fortunately my light was observed by the huge ship, which at once changed her course and bore past us. Had I been one minute later in putting up a light, every soul in the boat would have perished. Myself, and the rest of the boat's crew, were thus providentially saved from a watery grave by the interposition of my deceased wife.'

Sandwood Bay, some five miles south from Cape Wrath, in north-west Sutherland, is well-known for its ghostly associations. The Bay itself is a seven-mile stretch of sand dunes. Though bleak in wintertime, it is a beautiful spot in the summer months and a popular mecca for tourists seeking somewhere off the beaten track. The Bay is the haunting ground of a ghostly seaman. He has been sighted many times, but, when an investigation is made, there are no traces of footprints in the sand which would betray the presence of someone more substantial than a ghost.

Once, two men from nearby Oldshoremore were on the beach gathering driftwood. Suddenly, out of nowhere, the figure of a sailor in uniform appeared and commanded them to leave his property alone. Terrified, the men dropped their load of wood and fled from the spot. Some time later, a farmer from Kinlochbervie was out in the vicinity of the Bay with some of his men on the lookout for stray sheep. Darkness was beginning to fall before all the animals were rounded up and, as

The huge ship bears down on their small boat

the moon came out, the men noticed the outline of a tall man on the nearby rocks. Thinking it was one of the local men, they went towards the figure; but, as they drew near to him they realised that he was in fact a stranger and looked like a sailor. A few steps closer to him and the figure disappeared from their sight. A further search revealed nothing.

Several weeks after this incident, there was a severe storm off the west coast of Sutherland which caused an Irish vessel to go aground close by Sandwood Bay. A number of bodies were washed up on the beach and one of these was recognised by a local man (one of those who had been out looking for the sheep) as the sailor seen among the rocks. He was a heavily-built, black-bearded man. Since then, the mysterious sailor has regularly haunted the area.

Sandwood Cottage, nearby, has stood untenanted for many years as one of the most isolated and solitary habitations in Scotland. Many over-night campers have been disturbed by the figure of the seaman, with bearded face, peaked sailor's cap, and a tunic with brass buttons. One visitor to the cottage has had the experience of being wakened one night by the sensation of being suffocated by a thick, black mass that pressed down upon him. Even holiday-makers, who have camped overnight near the cottage, have not escaped the noises coming from the empty cottage of banging doors, windows being smashed and sounds of heavy footsteps in the building.

Fodderty Churchyard, in Ross-shire, on the way to Strathpeffer, is said to be the place where a ghost wanders each night among the graves, searching for that of her faithless lover. She is often seen wringing her hands and weeping. Those who see her are aware

Phantom sailor of Sandwood

She flies from the ghostly forms

of an eager questioning in her eyes as she makes attempts to approach them. It is said that if any person stays long enough for her to catch up with them, to answer her questions, will meet with misfortune; though if that person can tell the restless spirit where her faithless lover lies buried, he will reap a great reward.

Another churchyard with the reputation of being haunted is that beside the small church of Kiltarlity, near Glenconvinth, Inverness-shire. On one occasion, a woman was passing the church gate after dark on her way to visit a married daughter. Suddenly, she saw, as she thought, the daughter with her husband and baby waiting to meet her. Surprised, she pressed forward to meet them; they disappeared. The figures seemed to be in some distress when they reappeared. This time, the woman walked slowly towards them, but for every step she took, the figures kept their same distance from her. Puzzled, the woman happened to look to her left: the figures were there before her eyes; she looked to the right, and saw them there also. Realising that she was seeing ghostly forms, the woman turned and fled.

Shortly after this, the ghostly figures were also seen by a number of other people. In time the local minister took notice of this and decided to investigate the cause of the manifestations. One night he waited in the churchyard until long after midnight. His patience was rewarded by a light movement in the darkness. The figures appeared to him and, showing signs of distress, glided past to join the grey shadow of an old woman at a spot on the bank of the nearby river, which was notorious for flooding in springtime, with the waters often seeping into the churchyard. A thought struck the minister and he went into the church to look over the parish records. It was as he thought: some eighteen months previously a small part of the churchyard had been washed away in the flooding. The ground had contained three graves: those of a mother, her daughter who had died in childbirth, and the daughter's young husband, a wood-cutter who had been killed in an accident.

The following day, the minister organised a search along the river bank and soon a pile of bones was heaped up in the church porch. When the search had revealed all that could be found, a new funeral service was held and the bones duly given a Christian burial. A new headstone was erected, paid for by public subscription, for many desired to see the ghosts laid once and for all time. And so they were.

The ghostly figures are spotted again

PHANTOM OF THE SHINTY MATCH

The following unusual ghost tale has a South Uist setting. One New Year's Day, at Daliburgh, at the south end of the island, two rival shinty teams prepared for their usual annual contest. The *camanachd* was played with the skill and fervour associated with the game, until, towards the end, a dispute arose between the two team captains on a point of ruling. One of the captains, Iain, became so angry that he raised his club and was about to strike the other a heavy blow when his eye caught sight of a tall, well-built man in dark clothing approaching him at a quick walking pace. The man beckoned him to accompany him to the beach nearby. Iain was so seized by fascination that, without any hesitation, he left the field of play, while the members of both teams were overcome with no other desire than to leave the place in a hurry. All had felt somehow that the incident was more than unusual. Strangers in a small place are so noticeable; yet this man had never been seen before.

As the stranger approached, Iain noticed that his feet did not touch the ground, but seemed to glide over the small pebbles. Despite his reputation for fearlessness and courage, Iain began to tremble. But the stranger put him at ease by saying that he was, as Iain suspected, a ghost who had interfered with the dispute on the field of play. The man, when alive, represented a member of Iain's family, though this was the first time that Iain had seen his likeness. The ghost then required Iain to act as a contact between him and the living and required that Iain meet him frequently, promising misfortune if he should refuse.

From that day onwards, Iain was under a compulsion to meet the spectre. He tried to escape the ghost by moving to another part of the island, but to no avail. The ghost discovered him the next evening and exercised the same control over him as he had always done. What transpired between Iain and the ghost was never revealed. Except that one day Iain said to the others that the ghost had indicated that he would die in a house in a place which was then nothing but a mossy waste, without house or hut from end to end. Some years later, without any reference to what the ghost had forecast — for he had forgotten the incident — Iain did indeed build a house in the place mentioned and lived there to a ripe old age. The account of Iain and the ghost (Iain belonged to a well-known family in South Uist and his strange relationship was not unknown to his neighbours) was for many years after his death, one of the tales told round the fire. Even today, the incident is as yet only half forgotten.

One night a man named John was walking home to his native village of Laxay, from nearby Keose, in Lewis, when he arrived at a bridge crossing a small burn. He was about to step on the bridge when his eye caught sight of a strange light nearby. Thinking it was someone from his own village with a torch-light, he called out, but got no answer. He called out again and this time the response was a flaring of the light and its lengthening vertically to the height of a man. Again, thinking that someone was playing a trick, John called out a third time. No answer. So he went over to the light to grapple with

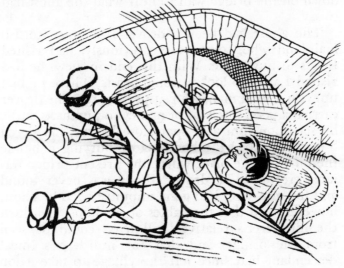

A struggle for John

it and was suddenly confronted by a large dark form which began to wrestle with him. Try as he might, John was unable to come to grips with his opponent, though his opponent's grip was not so uncertain. After a time, the struggle brought John near to the edge of the burn. As he lay on the ground, with the water gurgling in his ear, he, in a last desperate attempt for his life, managed to say: ' God have mercy on me! '

Instantly, his opponent relaxed the hold which had kept John firmly on the ground. As he recovered, John saw that he had been fighting with a ghost. Forced by the ghost's presence, John sat down on the bridge wall to hear what the ghost had to say.

The ghost had been a drover from the Scottish mainland who, some years previously, had visited Lewis to buy cattle. With this end in view, he had visited Laxay to look at some beasts. There he met up with a local man, who suspecting that the drover carried a good purseful of money to purchase cattle, he set upon him at a spot close by and murdered him. He robbed the body before burying it beside the burn, at the place where the present bridge was later erected. The drover's body was never found and the murderer had gone unpunished. The ghost, however, said that the gables of the house in which the murderer's relatives still lived could be seen from the bridge, and that the murderer's lineal descendant had since left the village to take a job on the Scottish mainland. After the encounter, John managed to make his way home and alarmed his own relatives, who were waiting up, by being violently sick as soon as he entered the house, and being confined to bed for a week with an illness which defied the local doctor's attempts to analyse.

While this story may seem to mirror some other tales about encounters with the ghosts of pedlars and similar itinerants, the family of John (a fictitious name) still lives in the neighbouring village of Keose.

The following story is of the Rev. Thomas MacKay, who was minister of Lairg, in Sutherland, and who, during his lifetime usually wore full clerical dress. He died in 1803. One summer's day in 1826, two young girls were sitting in the manse dining room when they heard a step advancing to the door. At once the door opened and they saw standing in the doorway a thin, old man, dressed in black, with knee breeches and buckles, black silk stockings and shoes with buckles. With a stare that took in everything in the room, he stood for a few moments and then walked out. After they had recovered from their astonishment, the girls mentioned the incident to the resident minister who, curious to know who his visitor was, searched the house, but found no one.

Some older people, having heard the girls' description of the old minister, knew it at once to be that of the deceased Rev MacKay. About ten years after this incident, the same two girls, having reached womanhood, met one of the Rev MacKay's grand-daughters; on seeing one of the grand-daughters, one of the women exlaimed: 'How like you are to your grandfather! ' To which the other replied: ' So the old people tell me, but how did you know that, for he died before you were born? ' The woman had in fact recognised the grand-daughter's resemblance to the old minister who had appeared to her in the manse.

A STRANGE ENCOUNTER

In 1869, a man from the parish of Farr, in Suther-land, had occasion to post a letter. It was a distance of over two miles to the post office, most of the way being across some hills. As he approached the main road, he was taken hold of by some unaccountable fear and a feeling of imminent danger. So alarmed did he become that he thought of turning back, though the day was bright and calm. Suddenly he was confronted by a man well known to him, whose face and hands were a mass of congealed blood. He asked the injured man what had happened to him, but was waved off. He, however, noticed that one of the man's fingers was broken.

The injured man told him that he had left his mother's house two days before, intending to visit some friends in a neighbouring village, and took a path which ran along the cliffs so as to shorten his journey. At the lower end of his mother's croft, which ran down to the cliffs, his foot slipped and he fell to the bottom of the rocks. He stated further that he had lain there for two days and two nights and that once he had heard, carried by the wind, his mother's voice as she spoke to a neighbour, who was helping her to cut some corn above the cliff. With a deep sigh, the ghost said: 'It was cruel of you to leave me there so long.' Then he vanished from sight.

The man, startled and still half-frozen with fear, hurried on his way and arrived at the post office

He falls down the cliff

Three spirits of the shipwreck

where it was seen that he was suffering from some kind of mental anguish. He was induced to tell the cause of his distress, and after some inquiries, the postmaster, in the company of the minister and others, hurried to the spot indicated. There they found the lifeless body of the man whose mysterious appearance had so terrified the other man. One side of the head was badly injured, and the middle finger of the left hand was broken. Everything was as described an hour before the body was discovered.

A well-to-do Shetland fishcurer once died rather suddenly. One morning, several days after the burial, his son entered the shop to be confronted by the figure of his father standing by the desk, apparently deep in the study of some accounts. He disappeared immediately. But later the same figure was seen by workmen in the deceased man's curing sheds.

The following indicates a common request by ghosts to be re-interred in places which are more comfortable. A boat on the west coast of Scotland was wrecked and three of her crew were drowned. The bodies were found and, according to custom, they were not carried to the churchyard but buried on the spot, near the scene of the wreck. Soon afterwards, three spirits were often seen to hover near the burial place. The local folk, determined to rid themselves of the apparitions, decided to disinter the bodies and found the graves full of water. After re-burial in dry earth, the apparitions were satisfied and never bothered the living in the district.

A similar story is told of a woman, from the same

district, whose spirit appeared to several folk, including her husband, a few days after her burial asking that her body be removed on account of the water that was collecting in her grave. The grave was opened and was indeed found to be full of water. A drain was constructed beneath the grave. The body was reburied and her ghost was never seen again.

The following story is yet another authentic instance of a sighting of a manifestation, and is probably more unusual for its sequel. A friend of the writer was employed in Stornoway, Lewis, to which town he made his way to work daily from the village of Grimshader, a few miles to the south of Stornoway. The road from the village crosses the southern part of Arnish Moor to meet the main Harris-Stornoway Road. For many years there had been a local tradition that the area near to the road junction was haunted, having been the scene of a murder. But there had never been anything substantial to confirm this tradition.

One evening, when B was returning from Stornoway, in a small van, he had no sooner turned off the main road onto the smaller Grimshader Road when he became aware of a spirit figure beside him; the face was indistinct, but there was no doubt about its supernatural character. The figure's presence remained for a mile or so, then disappeared. While one such experience was unnerving enough, the matter became quite depressing to B when he found that each night as he turned off the main road, the same ghostly manifestation accompanied him along for about a mile. Even when on a motor-bike, the figure would materialise and travel silently alongside. In the end, B resorted to a small boat with an outboard motor, to make the journey by sea to Stornoway, a distance of about five miles.

A few years ago, since when B had left Lewis for another part of the British Isles, a man's body was discovered near the junction of the Grimshader road with the main road to Stornoway. The find consisted of human remains, clothing and personal objects. Due to the action of the peat acid, the bones were reduced to the consistency of rubbery seaweed. The woollen cloth required several washings and then treated with a lanolin solution in order to replace lost fats in the material. The skeleton was that of a man of between 20 and 25 years of age. The opinion of the Department of Forensic Medicine, in Edinburgh University, was that ' . . . the appearances seen in the posterior part of the right parietal bone are consistent with, and indeed suggestive of a localised depressed fracture such as would result from the impact of an object having a defined striking surface. The position of this fracture would be consistent with a blow wielded by a right-handed assailant attacking from the rear.' Surely this could mean that the young man had been murdered. The clothing is dated c. 1700.

The local tradition is that two youths attending a school at Stornoway went to the moors on a bird-nesting expedition. They quarrelled when sharing out the spoil, and one of them felled the other by a blow on the head with a stone. When he realised that his companion was dead, he buried him and fled to Tarbert, Harris, whence he made his way to the south and took up a seafaring life. Many years afterwards his ship put into Stornoway and he went ashore, probably intending to remain incognito. But he was recognised, convicted of murder and hanged on Gallows Hill.

As often told, the story was provided with a dramatic denouement. On coming ashore from his ship, the guilty man entered one of the inns on the waterfront of the town and ordered a meal. While waiting for it to be served, he noticed that the handles of the cutlery on the table were of an unusual design. He was told that the handles were made from some sheep bones found in a hole on the Arnish Moor. He handles the cutlery and is terror-stricken when the bone handles ooze blood. This refers to the motif of the corpse beginning to bleed when touched by the murderer. For many years the scene of the murder was believed to be haunted and people avoided that particular stretch of the road after dark.

The ghost was often to be seen, particularly about four miles north of Soval, in the vicinity of a grey rock, white in part towards the top, near a little stream, on the right-hand side of the road coming back from Stornoway.

The body in the peat of Arnish Moor was found so near the scene of the almost legendary crime that it is not unreasonable to link the two. And that the man was murdered, there is little doubt. What remains, perhaps, to be explained is the reason for the spirit manifestation which confronted my friend. But, as seems to be the wish of most manifestations, the ghost merely desired to speak of the crime which deprived him of his life.

He orders a hearty meal

Spinning a thrilling yarn!

GHOSTS IN FOLKTALE
AND LEGEND

THAT the ghost has been an ever-present factor in the patterns of life and death in many rural areas and communities is seen in the large number of folktales and legends which feature a spirit of some kind or another and which have been in oral circulation for many centuries; only in the last century or so have they been recorded and written down. Some ghost tales of the Highlands and Islands are extremely old and have a thread of continuity which goes back at least one thousand years. In similar fashion, many localities have preserved stories and tales of ghosts. The Borders of Scotland have been a rich area of ballads, many of which feature the supernatural, perhaps in more dramatic form than the simpler folktale.

There is a small island called Hellisay, in the Sound of Barra, Outer Hebrides. The sea round its shores is full of fish, a fact which has never escaped the attention of the folk on nearby Eriskay island. One day an Eriskay man, his son and grandson set out for a day's fishing. After they had set their lines, they decided to make for Hellisay to explore the place. Once on the island the grandfather made off on his own, in the direction of an empty house which had belonged to a shepherd recently evicted from Hellisay. The other two stayed on the shore beside their boat.

Confrontation over a plank!

Looking in at one of the windows, the old man's eyes caught sight of a fine long plank of wood. As wood is a scarce commodity in the Hebrides where there are virtually no trees and the folk have to rely on what the sea throws up on the shores, he decided that it would be a good prize to take back with him to Eriskay. He managed to open the door, went into the house, gathered up the plank and made for the shore. But on the way back he was confronted by a ghost which tried to take the plank from him. The shape of the ghost was indeterminate but there was no doubt that if he wanted to keep the plank he would have to fight for it. A serious struggle followed.

In the meantime the father and son were sitting in the boat by the shore waiting for the old man to return. When he did not make an appearance, the son was told to go and look out for him. The boy did so and clambered over the high sand dunes. As he came close to the deserted house he saw his grandfather fighting with the ghost over the plank. With a spurt of sand-dust on his heels, the boy ran back to the boat, followed by his grandfather's words:

"Calum! Be as quick as you can! Tell your father to come here with the helm of the rudder. I'm here fighting with the Devil!"

"Grandfather is fighting with the Devil!" shouted the lad to his father.

"It's high time the Devil did come and take your grandfather — he should have taken him a long time ago!" was the reply from the father as he took the helm and made for the spot where the fight was going on with no ground being given or taken. As soon as the father came in sight, the ghost disappeared.

The old man sat down, apparently quite exhausted.

"Why did you not come sooner?" he asked. "I wanted to knock him one with the helm so that he'd never come back again."

But the plank, the prize, had been won, and the proud grandfather walked down to the shore with it. They were about to push off when another boat from Eriskay landed and some men from it came over to them. As they greeted them, they caught sight of the old man's plank of wood. Then they told the story of how they had searched Eriskay for a good plank of wood to make a coffin for a woman who had died the previous night. But they had not been able to find anything suitable. Now, eyeing the old man's plank, they asked if they could have it. He agreed and the plank changed hands. The Eriskay woman was put into the coffin and later buried. The Hellisay ghost was never seen again.

In some Highland ghost tales, the ghost is presented as a ghost of 'substance,' in that the figure appears as being no different from living men. Indeed, the more substantial the ghost, the older the tale seems to be; ghosts of more recent belief and origin tend to be ordinary, insubstantial and rather airy beings.

In a tale collected by J. F. Campbell, we are told of the many adventures of the 'Barra Widow's Son.' During his travels he arrived at one stage in Turkey and soon after met up with a strange sight, that of two men beating a corpse as hard as they could.

"What are you doing?" asked John, the widow's son.

"This man was a Christian. We had eight marks against him and since he did not pay us when he was alive we are taking it out of his corpse."

"Well, then. If you care to leave him with me I will pay you the eight marks."

The men, well satisfied, left John with the body. He, as the tale goes, 'put mould and earth on him'; that is, he committed the body to a decent grave and burial.

Many more adventures were to befall John after this incident before he found himself on his way home, sailing with his lady-love, the King of Spain's daughter. But the same ship carried a General who, jealous of John, managed by trickery to get John cast away on a desert island. In distress and despair, John thought his position quite hopeless, 'hair and beard grown over him; his shoes were worn to pulp, without a thread of clothes on that was not gone to rags; without a bit of flesh on him, his bones but sticking together.'

Eventually, just when he thought his end had come, he heard one night the sound of a boat rowing towards the island.

"Are you there, Iain Albannaich?" asked a voice.

Not a little afraid, for he was quite uncertain of what to expect, John went down to the shoreline and there found a man in a boat in the water's edge.

"What will you give me if I take you off this

desolate island? " John was asked. " Would you give me half your kingdom, half your wife and children? "

John answered that he had no kingdom, no wife and no children. But if he had he would most certainly give them to the stranger. Anything to get off the island.

" As good as done," said the stranger. So John and the unknown man rowed away to eventually land in Spain. There John in due course recovered his lady-love and was married. By this time the stranger had vanished as mysteriously as he had appeared and was all but forgotten when, after John had become the King of Spain and the father of three sons, he re-appeared once more to confront John.

" Are you for keeping your promise? " he asked.

" Yes," said John, who then prepared to make his sacrifice to keep his old bargain.

But the stranger said: " For your willingness you can have back what you were prepared to give me. I am the man for whose body you paid the eight marks."

So saying, he vanished from John's sight for all time.

There was once a widow who had an only son. She did not wish him to marry until it was her pleasure that he should do so, and he was persuaded to promise that he would seek her permission if ever he wished to marry. One day, when it was snowing hard, she killed a bird and asked her son to leave home and look for a girl whose cheeks were

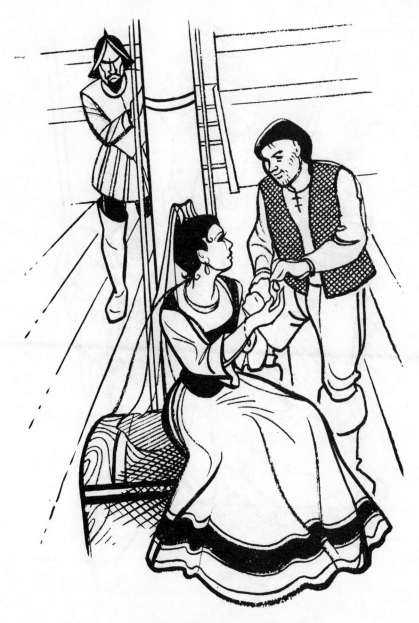

John is re-united with his lady love

Beating a corpse over unpaid debt

as red as the blood on the snow, who had skin as white as the snow and whose foot would fit a crystal shoe she had.

So the young man started out on his quest. On the first night away from home he passed a churchyard from which some strange noises were coming. Looking over the wall he saw some men breaking up bones. These were part of a man's skeleton. Asking why they were doing this, he was told that they had a debt against the dead man and were now taking their revenge. Offering the amount of the debt, the men revealed that they in fact were as dead as the skeleton whose bones they were breaking. But, they said, their brothers and sisters still lived and he could deliver the money to them.

This the young man did. Afterwards, on his way through a dark and lonely wood, he met a man who told him that it was for him the debt had been paid. Asking the son if there was anything he needed, the ghost-man was told of the quest for a girl who would satisfy his mother's description.

"You will be successful enough," was the reply, and the son then received direction to a house where he would obtain a cloak of darkness which, when worn, would render the wearer invisible. This was the start of many adventures, all successful and rewarding, thanks to the pity of the living for the bones of the dead.

On the west coast of Lewis, a fisherman's young wife was left alone one night while her husband went out fishing. During the night she heard strange cries which so upset her that she became afraid.

When she told her husband about them on his return he laughed at her and said that the cries were most likely those of seagulls. But she said she was convinced that the cries were such that no bird could have made them.

On the following night, when her husband had gone out fishing again, the young woman heard the cries and decided to find out their origin. Clutching her rosary of shells, she followed in the direction of the cries and came upon the ghost of a drowned foreign woman, whose body had been found on the shore and buried nearby.

The ghost told the woman that until her grave had been 'paid' for, she could never rest, and she would be condemned to wander for ever on the shore. The woman said that though hers was a very poor fisherman's family she would see what she could do to help.

"Cut a sheaf of ripe corn from your husband's field and lay it in my grave. Then I shall be able to rest."

The woman went off to get the corn, but wondered how she could open the grave. But on her return, however, she found the ghost standing by the grave, opened to receive the 'payment.' Placing the corn in the grave, the ghost thanked the woman and, taking a clear black stone from the folds of her dress, handed it to the woman.

"Keep this and give it to your son on the day he becomes seven years old."

Saying that, she lay down in the grave, which

closed over her, to leave the woman alone save for the sounds of the nearby waves on the shore.

Some months after this a son was born to the fisherman's wife and the ghost incident was forgotten. Years passed and it was not until the son's seventh birthday that the stone was remembered and given to the boy, who was later known as *Coinneach Odhar,* the famous Highland seer of Brahan.

Gift of a black stone

A minister in Skye had more concern during his lifetime for his cattle than for his parish flock of people. Even after he died his ghost was often to be seen hovering around the cattle-fold. There was much discussion about this nuisance, and it fell to one old man to volunteer and lay the troublesome spirit. One night he went to the fold and waited until he caught sight of the minister's ghost. Shouting a greeting and extending his hand, the ghost came towards him. But just as it was about to shake the old man's hand, the latter substituted an iron ploughshare. Touching the cold metal, the ghost disappeared and was never seen again.

There was once a ghost who caused no end of bother to people travelling on a particular road in Lochaweside, Argyll. In the end, in desperation, the word went out for someone strong enough and with the knowledge necessary to lay the spirit. One such man was found who went to the ghost's favourite haunting spot. There he met the ghost and exorcised it in the name of Peter and Paul and all the most powerful saints. But the ghost never moved. At last the call went out:

" In the name of the Duke of Argyll, I tell you to get out of there immediately! "

And the ghost promptly disappeared and was never seen again.

Get out!

GHOSTLY NOISES AND LIGHTS

It may well be that those who have never had the experience of seeing some visible ghostly manifestation are compensated either by seeing strange lights or by hearing noises the origins of which are quite unaccountable. Certainly, many have claimed to have seen lights and heard noises for which they could give no satisfactory explanation. But lights and sounds are often integral parts in the bag of tricks which the mind sometimes plays on us. The sun glancing on some bright object; the strange magnifying effects which people have seen from a boat looking to the landward sky to observe moving shapes almost mirroring some movement on the land hidden from seaward; the echoes of noises on a clear, still night originating a long distance away. All these have undoubtedly raised questions when their origins were claimed to be supernatural.

The growth of interest in Unidentified Flying Objects over the years has resulted in a large body of devotees willing to accept that the significant percentage of unexplained light-based objects seen in the sky is due to non-earthly, though not necessarily supernatural, manifestations. Whether they would accept a spirit explanation for the UFO is doubtful, being determined to subject their ' sightings ' to all kinds of tests with a scientific and rational base.

There is a fairly large body of accounts of ghostly lights and sounds which defy rational explanation, and which include such subjects as death divination and second sight. Usually the appearance of lights indicates the death or forthcoming death of someone either known to the seer or else someone in the community. One man, who was not given to story-telling for its own sake, took serious views about omens seen either by himself or by others. On several nights the sounds of a strange four-oared boat were heard coming from the opposite shore of Loch Erisort, Lewis, close by his home. This, he said, presaged a death, and the inevitable occurred within two months by the arrival of two boats, each bringing a coffin to the village. On a hillside near Loch Erisort a light was often seen which was taken as a sign of the proprietor's death. The event took place within the year. On many other occasions the lights of phantom boats were seen, all omens of forthcoming deaths which came about in due time.

One man in the village of Carnish, North Uist, related how he had heard strange rappings on the walls of his store for a period of several nights. He found the sound omen confirmed when some coffin furnishings were required from his shop soon afterwards.

But the fact can often play tricks on one's imagination. Damp, mossy peat banks sometimes exude a phosphorescent glow which can be mistaken for many things. This phenomenon is due to a small plant which is found in decaying vegetation and which is common in some parts of the moors in Scotland. If it is observed as being all over a person who is walking on the moor at night, it is taken for a sign of death by drowning at sea.

The late Alasdair Alpin MacGregor tells the story of a doctor from Edinburgh who was holidaying at an inn at Broadford in Skye. After supper he decided to take a turn outside before settling down for the night. Walking along the shore in the half-light of the evening, he noticed a glow out in the bay. At first he took it to be a flare lit by some fisherman in a boat. But then he noticed that the light was travelling too smoothly for that explanation. In addition, it was travelling at a pace which indicated that it was no ordinary kind of light. Gradually the light came nearer until it touched the shoreline — then went out. The next thing of which the doctor was aware was the form of a cloaked woman, with a child in her arms, hurrying across the sand in front of him. The glimpse he caught was only a fleeting one, because the woman vanished in a moment.

Returning to his lodgings, the doctor told his host of what he had seen and asked him for some possible explanation. With some reluctance he was told of a shipwreck, which had occurred several years before, in which a woman and child had been cast ashore, both dead, at the very spot at which the doctor had seen the strange light. This occurrence is said to be seen occasionally, even in these modern times, usually on or near the anniversary of the tragedy.

Another strange light is associated with Loch Rannoch. This takes the form of a glow in the shape of a ball which has been seen skimming across the surface of the water. It always rises from the same point, travels the same short distance, and disappears in the same place. Local tradition tells of those who have observed this same light not only on the water but rolling up from the loch to climb the nearby hill known as Meall-dubh.

Balls of light or fire are also known on Loch Tay. These are more specific in spirit origin and are related in connection with a man whose two brothers died of fever while he was serving in the Army. The brothers were buried in the churchyard at Kenmore. On the return of the surviving brother from active service, he decided to re-inter the remains at Killin, at the other end of Loch Tay. The night before the proposed exhumation, two very bright balls of fire were seen rolling along the surface of the water, in the very direction to be followed the next day by the boat containing the two coffins.

Highland tradition is full of tales of ghostly noises, of which the noise of phantom coffin-making is the most common. There was once a time when scarcely a carpenter's shop existed which did not have its full quota of sights and sounds seen and heard immediately before a coffin was made. These sounds invariably occurred at night and were heard either by the carpenter himself or by a member of his family. Wood intended for coffins is particularly noted to be troublesome about a house or shop. Wood is dashed to the ground; furnishings for coffins are apt to get noisy and restless; trestles are shifted about; and the noises of sawing, cutting and planes shaving wood are often heard.

Corpse candles are common sights. These 'candles' or lights are often seen flickering as they go along their way to the churchyard. If the lights are seen close to the ground, the omen is for an immediate funeral; if rather higher in the air, the funeral will not occur for some time. Corpse candles may be seen as long before a funeral as three months.

Near the shore at North Ballachulish there used to be a level spot of grounds, green and grassy, round which blackthorn bushes grew in something like a parallelogram form, as if they had been planted in that way. The spot was always held in terror by the local folk, who told of strange blue-flame lights being seen frequently around the place; it was a place to be avoided at nights. For a long time it was thought that the place marked the spot on an old chapel or religious cell. But a later investigation into old local records proved it to be a small area of ground set aside in olden times for the burial of unbaptised infants and suicides.

Father Allan MacDonald, parish priest of Eriskay at the turn of this century, recorded many aspects of folklore and traditions of the island of Eriskay and neighbouring South Uist. In particular, he recorded many valuable instance of ghostly, or at least inexplicable, happenings which defied attempts at rationalisation.

Both ghostly lights and sounds feature in his notes. He relates:

'Towards the end of August 1888 I was called to attend a dying woman at South Lochboisdale (South Uist). After administering the rites of religion, a crew and boat were procured. As we were nearing Strom Dearg, one of the rowers drew attention to a light playing on the shore just at the spot where we had embarked. It continued for some time, but its appearance did not cause much astonishment, only we could not imagine what objects any person would have in being in such a spot at such a time. We thought the dying woman would live till morning, but when the boatmen returned home, the woman was dead, and they were told that she was dead just at the time we should have been approaching Strom Dearg. The men spoke of the light and made diligent enquiry if any person had been to the shore, and it was found that no person was there. The coincidence was remarkable.'

Twice in his experience, a carpenter in South Uist, often engaged for the task of making coffins, told of observing ' a lamb surrounded with rays of light standing in the coffin.' These two occurrences took place when the coffin was in a dark part of the house.

Among the noises recorded by Father Allan are those heard at a spot in Eriskay known as *Glaic Charnan an t-Seirm*. These voices were often heard by the island folk at this place and a cairn of stones was set up. The sounds were taken as a *manadh* or warning, foretelling of future events. At one time Eriskay supported a very small population. This was later increased when some of the smaller islands in the Sound of Barra were cleared of crofters, many of whom made their new homes on Eriskay. As Father Allan remarks: 'And there was little wonder that voices should be heard, considering that so many people were to come to stay in the island afterwards.'

About 1870, some boys were playing on a little beach near *Coilleag a' Phrionnsa* (the Prince's Strand, where Prince Charles Edward landed in 1745). It was in the wintertime, with a fine, clear moon shining from a dark sky. After some time, a passing cloud darkened the beach and the boys stopped playing, to rest a while beside a sandhill. Suddenly their dog, which had been previously running about happily chasing the boys' ball, cowered in terror and lay close to the ground. His hair stood erect and he appeared to be in great terror. At the same time as the boys noticed the dog's curious behaviour, they heard a very loud noise, a rumbling and a crashing as though many iron plates were being dragged over the nearby rocks down to the shore. The boys' immediate reaction was to scamper home as fast as they could — which they did, with the dog not far behind thcm. Father Allan comments that the lads 'were not philosophical enough to examine into possible natural causes for the occurrence.'

Another sound of supernatural origin is associated with Cottertown, near Auchenasie, Keith, Aberdeenshire. It was connected with a murder and is related by Walter Gregor in his book *Folk-lore of the North East of Scotland*:

'On the day on which the deed was done, two men, strangers to the district, called at a farmhouse about three miles from the house in which lived the old folk that were murdered. Shortly before the tragic act was committed, a sound was heard, passing along the road the two men were seen to take, in the direction of the place at which the murder was perpetrated. So loud and extraordinary was the noise that the people left their houses to see what it was that was passing. To the amazement of everyone, nothing was to be seen, though it was moonlight so bright that it aroused attention. All believed something dreadful was to happen, and some proposed to follow the sound. About the time discussion was going on, a blaze of fire arose on the hill of Auchenasie. The foul deed had been accomplished and the cottage set on fire. By the next day we all knew of what the mysterious sound had been the forerunner.'

In Nigg Bay, Easter Ross, there is said to be a sunken village and church. The local tradition was that if anyone heard the sound of the church bell from the sunken spire it foretold a death. Once a boat of fishermen went out into the bay for a spot of quiet fishing. All was peaceful with only the occasional comment between the fishers when one man suddenly looked startled and told his fellows he had just heard bells. With a great speed, the lines were hauled up and the boat was put back into port, all the men believing it to be a death omen for the man who heard the sound. And, indeed, the same man was found drowned three days after the incident.

Early this century, corpse candles or lights were often seen hovering about the Holly Pool, near Taagan, Wester Ross. They were seen for a number of years and only disappeared when two young children were found drowned in the pool, apparently after trying to negotiate it to get to an adjoining harvest field.

One day about eighty years ago, a man stood behind the schoolhouse at Dunmore and looked across West Loch Tarbert in the direction of the ferry plying between Port a' Chaolain, on the Kintyre side of the loch, and Ardpatrick, on the South Knapdale side. As he took in the scene he became aware of a light emerging from the roof of the ferry-house at Port a' Chaolain. It was about seven feet high and was bright enough to be seen at the distance involved, about two and a half miles. The next day the ferryman died.

One ghostly light led to the discovery of a link with a murder which had taken place almost two centuries previously. This occurred on the west coast of Lewis, near the crofting township of Carloway. Local tradition had always related the story of the Irish pedlar who met with his death in a very cruel manner after visiting a house at which he called to ask for directions to get to the next township. The man of the house, thinking that the pedlar would have a well-filled purse, offered to act as a guide. Thanking him for his charity, the pedlar and his guide started off. They had gone only a short distance when the guide turned on the pedlar and cruelly beat him to death. After the killing, the murderer, conscience-stricken, sought to hide the body and the pedlar's goods and purse. The former he buried in soft peaty soil. The latter objects he threw into an old disused well.

In due time, people of the village told each other of the strange light which they saw at nights, and always associated with the same area of ground. For many subsequent generations the light was seen and the story of the pedlar's murder eventually passed into the realm of folktale. But, in 1922, some young men who had themselves often seen the mysterious white light, decided to investigate. One night they followed the light at a comfortable distance and noted carefully the exact spot at which it disappeared. Now, while tradition had always said that the light tended to hover over the old well, in fact the light went out beside it. The men then began to dig around the well and, with an increasing sense of anticipation, found an old and rotten sealskin purse containing a number of Irish pennies. The dates on most of the coins were by then undecipherable, but three bore dates of 1740, 1743 and 1744. Just as strange as the ghost light is the fact that since the coins were uncovered, the light itself has never been seen since.

One night, two farmers were jogging their way

home just outside Stornoway, Lewis. Arriving at a cross-roads, one of the men descended from the horse-drawn trap to make his own way home. Turning round to wave his friend good-night, he noticed that a strange light was hovering in front of the trap. The next day he asked his companion if he had seen the light. Indeed, the man had, and in fact had whipped up his pony in an effort to catch up with it. Two days later a farmer was drowned in Stornoway harbour. And his body was carried home in the same trap as the two companions had used only two days before.

In the island of Luing another light was once seen, this time by a man who followed the bright shape until it vanished over a rough-stone bridge, which was crudely made but was strong enough to carry the weight of a horse and loaded cart. He related the incident to his neighbours, who could give no explanation, except that it was obviously some kind of omen. The following morning, the son of a local farmer was returning home on the horse he had just shod at the local smithy. No more than half way across, the bridge suddenly collapsed and rider and mount were thrown into the stream. The horse fell on the rider and its weight pinned him under. He was drowned.

The island of Benbecula is noted for its angling, particularly the trout which abound in its many lochs. During the summer of 1938 a strange light was seen hovering over Loch Olavant; this light persisted for several consecutive days. Those who saw it were convinced that it was a portent of some kind. On the day following the last appearance of the light, an angler, not an islander, who had for many years favoured angling holidays on Benbecula, had a heart seizure while he was investigating a tiny island in the loch for birds' nests. The light was described as ' a glowing fire like a smouldering peat on the little island . . . and there was nothing to account for it.'

There are many sites of shielings in the Outer Hebrides and, being remote from inhabited townships, they are associated with tales of wonder and horror. Most of these are legends and folktales. But there are some of less doubtful origin. One story tells of a mysterious light which was seen persistently for about half a century near Leuchan, in Harris. As late as 1944 it was seen by several people who, thinking it was a signal of some kind, hurried to the spot. But when they arrived at the place, the light had disappeared. Marsh gas has been suggested but the local folk put a different interpretation on the light.

Another light is still seen in the township of Manish, also in Harris. The light has been observed by many people, always above a particular house. The real mystery surrounding this particular light is not so much in the light itself but in the fact that there is nothing unusual either about the site of the house or the history of the building.

In 1949 two friends were enjoying a pleasant evening together close by Loch Duntelchaig, a few miles from Inverness. As the dusk pressed in on them, they went into their car to finish off their conversation and their sandwiches. As they talked they became aware of a strange light hovering about ten feet in front of the car bonnet. One of the men turned the switch for the car headlamps, thinking he had left them on. But in fact the lamps were off. The light persisted for some time before it slowly faded away. Puzzled, the men got out to investigate, but found absolutely nothing.

On the west coast of the island of Barra, Outer Hebrides, two elderly sisters were preparing for bed after an extremely hard day in their small village store. One of the sisters was deaf, so much so that even a gun-shot made little impression. By the time they had made up their accounts, and saw to the ordering of more stores it was nearly two a.m. They tumbled into bed with the prospect of a good and full night's sleep in front of them. Towards the early hours of the morning, both sisters sat up in bed, startled, and the deaf one asked what was the terrible noise she had heard. Or had she only dreamt it? Her sister, thinking to comfort her, said it was only rats, though, ' I knew fine it was a loud knock on the window pane. I went and undid the door and felt with my hands round the house, it being very dark. There was nothing and nobody, and the night was dead silent, not even the sea making a murmur. So I went back to bed and to sleep. The next night, and it was at the very same time, we were wakened again by the loud knock, a ringing hard knock on the window so that you would wonder that it did not break the glass. And she (the deaf one) heard it the same as me. I rose again, but there was no one there. The third night I lay awake for I kenned fine I was needed. It came at the same time once more, and this time the deaf one did *not* hear. A soft, quiet knock on the pane and up I got and out. And there, crouching beside the window, was Sandy MacLean, sobbing like to break his heart.'

The lad had come to the store for the winding sheet for his mother who had just died.

At the turn of the century in Tiree, an old woman lay on her death-bed and while the rest of the household sat up with her, the youngest member, a lad, was packed off to his bed. Through the night he heard what he took to be the trampling of dogs in a loft above his sleeping place, and this he heard so distinctly that he asked his father next day what made him put the dogs there. The answer he got was that there were no dogs in the loft. The lad also heard a plank sliding down from the loft and striking on end in the passage between the doors. The following night the old woman died, and the lad himself was sent up to the loft to bring down planks to make her coffin. A plank slipped from his hands and, falling on its end in the passage, made exactly the same noise as he had heard the night before.

Horse and rider were thrown into the stream — see story on ghost light at Luing.

STRANGE HAPPENINGS

FOR every person who has genuinely seen a ghost, there are many more who have been witness to some strange occurrence which has defied rational explanation. Mysterious happenings include divination of death, the hearing of voices, seeing ghostly armies and so on, all of which tend to add credence to the existence of another world operating on a fluctuating time-scale and contemporaneously with our own rather time-fixed world.

South of Inverness there is a chain of attractive lochs which are harnessed to provide the town of Inverness with its water supply. One of these lochs is Loch Ashie. Close by are several cairns and tumuli and a large boulder (at the loch's north-western end) popularly known as King Fingal's Seat. It is said that a battle once took place on the moor in the immediate vicinity, between Fionn, or Fingal, and the men of Lochlann (Norway) who were led by their leader, King Ashie. Tradition has it, and a number of people living now have confirmed the tradition, that soon after dawn on May Day a ghostly battle is seen in progress between the two factions.

At the beginning of the 1870s, the battle was clearly observed by several people. It was thought at the time to be a trick of light which projected onto the Inverness moor a mirage of men fighting in a battle in the then progressing Franco-Prussian War. But as the images were seen after that war had ended, people sought to look for other explanations. During the First World War a cyclist in the area met up with three men walking along in front of him. To

Phantom soldiers

his amazement, he cycled right through them, and when he turned round he was even more amazed to see the traditional phantom armies in close formation fighting for their lives.

Another ghostly battle has been seen in Glen

Shiel. The original was fought in 1719 between the King's troops under General Wightman and a force of Spaniards who had landed in the west to help the Old Chevalier. The King's troops were victorious. On suitable nights the battle has been re-enacted with ghostly men, not only fighting, but beating a weary retreat up the Pass, and men on both sides silently burying their dead.

The bloody deeds of a nation's history burn deep into the mind and remain as fresh as though they were yesterday's occurrences. This is the case with the Forty-Five: the battlefield at Culloden sees over a hundred thousand visitors each year, many of whom are Scots and expatriate Highlanders who pay a kind of pilgrimage to the scene which sparked off a trail of death, disaster and humiliation for the Highlanders and their kith and kin. One story of the Forty-Five centres round a well on the road from Uig to Portree. It is known locally as Prince Charlie's Well. On the 15th of April 1746 the ghost of a tall young man was seen in its vicinity, with a sad and mournful expression on his face, and muttering in a voice that was heard by some people: 'Defeated, defeated, defeated.' The ghost then vanished from sight and the whole thing was taken as an omen of disaster. Suddenly, and without any warning at all, a ghost army was seen with arms clashing and drums beating. This sight also vanished. On the following day, the 16th of April, 1746, the Battle of Culloden was fought, and the forces of the Prince were defeated and scattered over the whole of the Highlands. Shortly afterwards, the fugitive Prince himself slaked his thirst at that same well. This was one of the many incidents recorded in the Highlands when coming events were foretold by the sighting of sad shadows.

Thirsty prince

Near the little picturesque village of Dores, on the eastern side of Loch Ness, there is the Well of the Phantom Hand. This is said to be the home of an extra-large spirit whose outstretched hand is sometimes to be seen reaching out over the heads of those about to drink from the well's waters. Many thirsty travellers have been terrified of the sight, but remained unharmed. The well has been associated with this tradition for the past two hundred years.

Many years ago in South Uist there was a house in which lived a family with a girl of seven who was dumb from birth. One night the old man in the house died and, pending the funeral arrangements, the corpse was laid on a suitable broad plank of wood. His son, the girl's father, left the house in the care of his wife and daughter while he went in search of a priest. He had not been gone long when suddenly the girl, who had never spoken a word in her life, said, '*Tha mo sheanair ag eirigh*' (my grandfather is rising).

Startled, the mother replied, 'If these are your first words of speech it is like we were not here,' and she took herself and the child into a small back room and barricaded the door with two heavy quern-stones and other suitable articles.

Not before time, it seemed, for the corpse rose from its plank and tried to push the room door open. Finding this impossible, it then began to dig under the doorpost with its nails. It was almost half-way through when the cock crew and the corpse stiffened. It was found in this position when the son returned.

The body was immediately placed in a coffin and was found to be extraordinarily heavy. The weight was so great that it put a severe strain on those who were carrying the bier. Then, not far from the graveyard, the weight suddenly lifted and the coffin became obviously the container of an ordinary corpse. This incident is supposed to have occurred at the latter end of the 18th century and is still told in South Uist.

It is often said that one of the most common reasons for a ghost's appearance is an attempt to right certain things which were left undone in life, or else to repay some kind of debt that might have been in the mind at the moment of death. In the Proceedings of the Psychical Society there is the story of a priest who reports as follows:

'In July 1838 I left Edinburgh to take charge of the Perthshire missions. On my arrival in Perth I was called on by a Presbyterian woman, Anne

Simpson, who for more than a week had been in the utmost anxiety to see a priest. This woman stated that a woman lately dead, named Moloy, slightly known to Anne Simpson, had appeared to her during the night for several nights, urging her to go to the priest, who would pay a sum of money, three and tenpence, which the deceased owed to a person not specified.

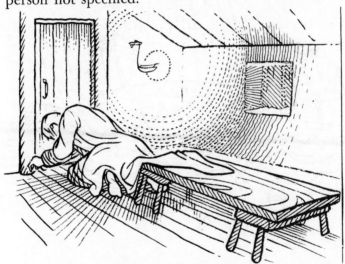

The corpse digs under the door

'I made enquiries, and found that a woman of that name had died and who had acted as washerwoman and followed the regiment. Following up the inquiry, I found a grocer with whom she had dealt, and on asking him if a female named Moloy owed him anything, he turned up his books and told me that she did owe him three and tenpence.

I paid the sum. Subsequently the Presbyterian woman came to me, saying that she was no more troubled.'

As might be expected, the island of Iona figures in many stories of strange sightings and experiences. Inside the Abbey itself, ghostly chanting of monks has been heard, and the monks themselves, or, rather, their centuries-old spirits, have been seen in slow procession in the vicinity of the Abbey. One woman has recorded her sighting of a monk: ' I saw him clearly with mental vision — so vividly that I'd

know him at once if I saw him again. Very gentle
and benign he was. He wore a brownish robe, and a
hempen rope round his waist; and there was a halo
round his head.'

Startled by the Viking longboats

On another occasion, a man was walking over a
part of the island which he knew like the back of
his hand. As he walked, however, he became slowly
aware that the scene before his eyes was strange and
one which he failed to recognise. In a growing state
of confusion he walked over to the White Sands.
No sooner had he arrived when he noticed a fleet
of Viking longboats emerge from behind a small
islet, *Eilean Annraidh*, 'fourteen long, thin boats

with high stems.' As he continued to look at this uncanny sight, he saw the boats land on the shore. Out of these leapt armed men who fell on a group of monks nearby. These they quickly dispatched before making off in the direction of the Abbey. Shortly afterwards, still seeming to be fixed in a time long past, the onlooker saw the returning men loaded with booty boarding their ships and push off from the White Sands.

As his time-slip brought him back to his own time and hour he found he could recall some of the emblems which he had seen emblazoned on the longboats' square sails. These were later verified by authorities as belonging to the late tenth century.

Another person who was witness to a similar occurrence on Iona was the late F. C. B. Cadell, the Scottish artist. A year or so before he died in 1938 he was painting near the Hermit's Cell when he found himself surrounded by fighting men of an obvious ghostly nature. The vision so disturbed him that he packed up his easel and paints and left the spot. He recorded later that he was puzzled by the fact that the knees of the warriors were on the level of the ground. This point could be explained in that during the intervening centuries the ground level might well have risen a foot or so.

A hooded maiden has often been seen on Loch Craignish, in the valley of the River Barbreck, between Ardfern and Ford. She is reported as having long hair which surrounds a very pale face. She is usually seen sitting on a rock dressed in an unspecified tartan. A hood hides most of her features. Her significance or import has never been discovered.

Mystery maiden

The home of Sir Walter Scott during the last twenty years of his life was his beloved Abbotsford. He was very interested in all forms of the occult and anything unusual and mysterious attracted him. One of his own personal experiences he duly recorded. This took place in the year of 1818, during some alterations in the building. Sir Walter remarked on a 'violent noise, like drawing heavy boards along the new part of the house.' The following night, at about 2 a.m., the same noises were heard again. Sir Walter investigated, accompanied by " Beardie's Broadsword," but was never able to discover the reason for the noises. At that time, however, the agent who was responsible for the alterations at Abbotsford died suddenly. The incident of the noises and the untimely death cannot but seem to be connected in some way.

Towards the latter end of the last century, a number of people on Eriskay were startled to hear coming from the direction of nearby Lingay Island cries as though a boatful of people were in sore distress. The cries were so real that a boat was immediately put out from Eriskay. After this boat had gone for some time, the cries stopped. The boat slowed down and those in her listened in silence. But nothing was heard. The crew were on the point of returning to land when the noises started once more. The craft was turned round and made off in the general direction from which the cries seemed to come. But again, before much headway had been made, the noises stopped. Each time the boat stopped and the crew decided to return to land, the cries began. In the end, thoroughly confused, the crew turned finally and made for home. The cries had been heard quite distinctly by all the crew. A thorough investigation carried out later revealed no sign of any wreckage and the whole matter remained a mystery. About eight years after the incident, an Eriskay boat struck on a rock near Lingay and, though the crew members were saved, they were nearly drowned.

Instances of second sight are numerous, particularly in the Highlands where the 'gift' is seemingly possessed by many people who prefer to keep their faculty in obscurity; and perhaps they are right to do so for fear of causing unnecessary distress to themselves and to their friends and neighbours. At the turn of this century a woman lived on a farm tucked away in the Rannoch hills. This woman was known to have been descended from a long line of women who had the 'gift.' One evening, after market day at Aberfeldy, a farmer was making his way home along the banks of the River Tay. In the gathering darkness he slipped and fell into the waters and was drowned. When he had not arrived home the following morning, his wife called out searchers to look for him, but they looked in vain. The river was dragged and re-dragged for almost three weeks and with nothing found but a hat and stick. The missing man's family were by this time in deep sorrow and were distressed by the thought that the missing man was not to have a Christian burial. But for that a body had to be found. The family visited the woman at Rannoch, whom they thought might be able to help them by her using her gift. Now this woman had never seen Aberfeldy and knew nothing of either the district or the people. But she concentrated on her task and eventually she reported that in some kind of a dream, during which she claimed she was not asleep, she saw a dead man in a reclining position, kept down by some tree roots at the ' bottom of a bridge, at the side of a river, below a queer bridge.'

The relatives of the missing man were at first confused by the ' picture' the woman had seen. It was all too vague. However, the reference to the ' queer ' bridge gave them a clue. They sketched the

Aberfeldy Bridge and showed it to the woman, who recognised it at once.

'That is the bridge,' she said. 'And the hole below it is at the side.'

'But we have dragged that part in vain.'

'I can't help that,' she said, 'the body is there now.'

So a search party went off with a boat and grappling irons to the spot indicated and began a further search. In a short time the body of the missing and drowned man was recovered, just as the woman at Rannoch had 'seen' it.

There is another story which centres on the same area and the same woman. A shooting tenant of an estate in Rannoch took a lad of the district back with him to England to have him trained as a groom. Shortly afterwards news came back to Rannoch that this lad had disappeared and could not be found. The woman with the 'gift,' already mentioned, was appealed to for help. At first the appeal was thought to be hopeless, for she had never been to England in her life.

But she persevered and eventually 'saw' first that the young lad had been murdered and buried among stones in a quarry near where he lived. This was not all, however. Scarcely had she seen all this than she 'saw' the murderers move the body from the quarry and fling it into a lake. The search for the lad commenced in England. Sure enough, a hole was found near the quarry and signs that many stones had been disturbed. Then the lake nearby was dragged and the Rannoch lad's body duly found.

At the beginning of the last war, the Committee for the Recording of Abnormal Happenings in Edinburgh received a letter from a woman who had had an unusual experience in August 1936 while she was at Culloden. She was wandering around the Highlanders' graves. 'Whether I was sufficiently steeped in atmosphere, I do not know; but certainly, when I lifted a square of Stuart tartan, which was blown down from the stone to the mound which is the grave, I distinctly saw the body of a very handsome dark-haired Highlander lying, as it were, at ease, on top of the mound.'

Realising that she was in fact seeing things and that the body was not a reality, except perhaps in the time of its own existence, two centuries previously, she fled from the spot.

Late in 1945 a man from Castle-Douglas was cycling home one night when he saw a light in front of him which he took to be a camp fire. As he approached the spot, he saw indeed a number of tinkers grouped round the fire with three or four horse-drawn caravans close by. He stopped and watched the scene for a moment, then made for home. It was not until afterwards that it crossed his mind that, though he had seen the encampment, he had heard no noise. The next morning, his mind full of curiosity, he cycled to the place where the camp should have been. But he found nothing: no tracks, no spent fire, no wheel marks, no marks of horses. What he had seen was a phantom tinkers' encampment.

Lost in the storm

The story is still told and sung in the Western Isles of Allan Morrison and Annie Campbell. Allan was the son of a Stornoway merchant and was a noted sea captain. He generally traded with his ship between Stornoway and the Isle of Man. One morning in the spring of 1786 he left Stornoway to go to the island of Scalpay to see his betrothed, Annie, and to go through the ceremony of the marriage contract with her. But a furious storm blew up and Allan's ship was swamped. All the crew were lost and Annie Campbell grieved for her lost lover for many days until she herself died in utter despair.

Her body was placed in a coffin and taken on board a ship for burial at Rodel, at the southern tip of Harris. On the passage, that vessel, too, was overtaken by a violent storm during which the coffin was swept overboard into the raging seas. At the same moment as this occurred, it was claimed that a form was seen, supposed to be that of Allan, who bore it away into the depths of the sea. Shortly afterwards, Allan's body was found at the Shiant Isles in the Minch. And a few days later Annie's own body was found at exactly the same place. This event is well known in the Gaelic west, and the song *Ailean Duinn* has been known and sung for generations to commemorate the way in which the two lovers were eventually united in death.

Many years ago, in Skye, one of the annual Fairs was to be held in Portree. Shortly before the Fair was due, a young woman of the district of Kilmuir, about eighteen miles from Portree, was found in a state of depression, lamenting the catastrophe which she said would soon take place; a boat sinking in a storm in which many people drowned. At the time, people put this down to a dream or some other such occurrence and was duly forgotten. Later, on the evening of the market-day, a large boat left Portree for Kilmuir, crammed with people anxious to get home. But a storm rose up and all in the ship were consigned to a watery grave.

The following is an authenticated account of an experience in Kirriemuir, at the turn of this century:

' As I passed the house, what looked like a piece of diaphanous material appeared from the top of a *closed* window and disappeared rapidly upwards. I learned later that a newly-born child died in that room of the house at that time . . . '

One man claims that he owed his life to a ghost. He was living at the time in Forres, and his experience happened while he and a friend were looking for a farm which lay about ten miles east of Elgin.

It was an evening in late autumn and both men left about seven o'clock on their bicycles, without lamps. After they had travelled some miles along a country road, they found themselves quite lost. In any case, the darkness had fallen quicker than they had expected and they decided it was better to turn back. This they did, and as they came to the top of a steeply descending road one of the men said he would go forward alone and ask his friend to follow after a short interval, to avoid any collision or accident.

" I then went on alone, and was half-way down when a light suddenly appeared at the left-hand side of the road. I jumped off my bike and stared at this unexpected phenomenon. It was a thin column of light about six feet in height. While I stood there wondering, the light flickered for a few seconds and then vanished as mysteriously as it had appeared.

" A few minutes later I heard my friend approaching and shouted to him to dismount. When he did so, I explained my reason for stopping and standing there half-way down, when he would naturally have expected to find me at the foot of the hill. We then searched around for some time but found no natural explanation to account for this light. There were only green fields on both sides of the road and no animals, no dwellings within miles and no marshes where " marsh lights " might appear. After our fruitless search I suggested that we walk down the remainder of the steep road, and it was a lucky thing we did so. When we reached the bottom of the road we found a small stone bridge at right angles to the road. But for the warning light we must both have crashed over the bridge and sustained serious, if not fatal, injuries.'

The strange case of Sergeant Davies's ghost is recorded in the annals of Scottish legal history. The year was 1749, when, despite three years of military subjugation, the Highlands had not yet been pacified. The spirit of the clans was abroad, and though the hills might seem lonely at first glance, in fact they were alive with people hiding from the soldiers and skulking in caves, hollows and the wooded parts of the glens.

One evening in the summer of 1749, Sgt. Davies, of Guise's Regiment, marched from Aberdeen to Dubrach, in Braemar, with a party of eight privates. The business of the party was to conduct general surveillance in the district and particularly to obtain information of any disaffected persons who might be hiding in the district. The sergeant was a popular man, well-liked and newly married. His wife was to later bear witness to the fact that " he and she lived together in as great amity and love as any couple could do, and that he was never willing to stay away a night from her."

On the 28th September Sgt. Davies and his party met up with John Gowar in Glenclunie, who was wearing a tartan coat. This was, of course, at that time proscribed dress and Davies advised him not to use it in public. He then dismissed Gowar rather than take him prisoner. Shortly after this incident, Davies left his men to try for a shot at a stag he had spied. He was never seen again. His men searched for him in vain. Later, with a much enlarged search party, the hills in the area were scoured. But no trace of the missing sergeant was found.

In the following year, 1750, a shepherd, Alexander MacPherson, made it known that he was " greatly troubled by the ghost of Sergeant Davies, who had insisted that he should bury his bones "

MacPherson was instructed by the ghost to contact a Donald Farquharson, with whom Davies had lodged. MacPherson did so, and with Farquharson's help and acting on information given by the ghost, the sergeant's bones were eventually found in a peat moss. The ghost still appeared to MacPherson, however, and gave him to understand that two men were responsible for his death, one Duncan Clerk and one Alexander Bain MacDonald. Again, acting on the ghostly information, these two men were arrested in September 1753 and held in the Tollbooth, Edinburgh, on various charges, including that of the wearing of the kilt.

In the following year they were tried, and evidence was produced which proved that the men had indeed killed the sergeant. But the case for the defence was stronger and the two men were acquited. Thus, for all its trouble, the ghost of Sergeant Davies failed to get final satisfaction.

Another equally strange incident is firmly lodged

in legal history. This time it concerned the death of a pedlar, whose murderer was finally convicted on the evidence of a man who had dreamed of the place where the dead man's pack was lying and which was needed as material evidence in the case for the prosecution.

The pedlar's name was Murdock Grant and at the time of his death he was tramping round the district of Assynt, in Sutherland, selling his goods: silk handkerchiefs, prints, cottons and worsted stockings. The month was March and the year was 1830 when news came to the parish minister that the body of a pedlar had been found in a nearby loch. At first sight it seemed as if the pedlar had fallen in by accident, but investigation showed that the body had sustained wounds feloniously produced. Further investigation led to the arrest of one Hugh MacLeod, a native of Assynt, who was later taken to Inverness for his trial. He faced two charges. The first was the murder of the pedlar; the second was the theft of £30 in bank notes, a purse containing £6 in silver and the pedlar's pack.

The most damning evidence against MacLeod was his possession of a large amount of money which was unaccounted for. At the conclusion of the Crown's evidence with regard to this money came the most extraordinary testimony of the whole trial. This was given by one Kenneth Fraser, known as The Dreamer, who said that he had a number of times after the date of the pedlar's death been a drinking partner with MacLeod. He told the court of his dream, through which the pedlar's missing pack was found:

"I was at home when I had the dream in the month of February. It was said to me in my sleep by a voice, like a man's voice, that the pack was lying in sight of the place (where the murder took place). I got a sight of the place just as if I had been awake. I never saw the place before, but the voice said in Gaelic the pack of the merchant is lying in a cairn of stones in a hollow near to their house. When the officer came, I took him to the place I had got a sight of. It was on the south-west side of Loch Tor-na-eigin. We found nothing there, and we then went to search on the south side of the burn. I had not seen this place in my dream, but it was not far from the place I had seen in my dream that the things were found. There were five silk handkerchiefs."

This evidence, given by The Dreamer, concluded the case for the prosecution and, when the trial ended, a jury returned their verdict of guilty as libelled. On Monday, October 24, 1831, Hugh MacLeod was hanged in Inverness for the murder of the pedlar. Before a crowd of seven thousand or so onlookers, he confessed his guilt as he stood on the scaffold.

Late last century a minister went to visit a brother of his, a Captain MacLeod, who lived near Portree, Skye, and who had been ill for some time. After his visit he returned home, but the weather turned bad and he decided to lodge the night with a Mrs Nicolson at Scorriebreck. Her house was one of the larger houses on the island, with trap-stairs to the upper flats where all kinds of lumber were usually stored. In one corner of this attic was deposited the parish mort-cloth, kept there for safety and for convenience as the parish burial-place was nearby. Once her guest had been welcomed and settled in, Mrs Nicolson went up into the attic room to fetch some things and left her guest with her family in the parlour. They were startled to hear a loud scream, followed by the noise of a fall. They rushed to the upper floor with a light to find Mrs Nicolson in a fainting fit and quite insensible. She later recovered and told the minister that as she was in the attic she became aware of a brilliant light on the mort-cloth, which was spread over a table. In the middle of the light she saw the distinct image of his niece's face, the daughter of his brother, Captain MacLeod.

The story caused some concern at first, but was then forgotten — until shortly after when the young lady whose image had been seen took to her bed with an illness and died. Her bier was the first to require the use of the mort-cloth in question after that strange incident.

Face of his niece

TALES OF HORROR

WHILST many ghosts tend to operate in their own time in the past, and almost ignore the living person who observes them, there are some which seem able to project themselves into another time, the present, and exhibit signs of malevolence towards those whom they meet. Whether the malevolence is intentional or not, there are many who have recorded their experiences which almost put fictional ghost stories to shame for their false inventions. The following stories have been collected from many sources over various parts of Scotland and serve to indicate the rather terrifying experiences of those persons who had the misfortune to come into contact, often unintentionally, with the spirits of the long-dead.

There are a number of haunted houses in Glasgow. Most of these were buildings in which have occurred such deeds as murders and suicides. Here, in fact, may lie the reason for the seeming malevolence of some ghosts which seek some kind of vengeance on the present living for the sufferings they had to endure at the hands of another living person in their own time-scale.

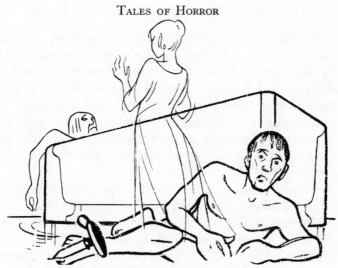

Horror in bathroom

One particular house in the neighbourhood of Blythswood Square in Glasgow was many years ago the subject of interest from a prospective buyer. He was taken with the whole building — except for the bathroom. This room struck him as being excessively grim; its atmosphere and general appearance upset him, though for what reason he could not say. It was a room, he recorded later, that he would prefer to remain outside when in the house by himself. In the event, his wife being so taken with the house, it was purchased, but not before the bathroom had been thoroughly modernised and painted, with a new, gleaming white bath surrounded by wood.

But even with this alteration, the owner felt decidedly uncomfortable whenever he was in the bathroom; this although other members of his family felt nothing at all. The owner compromised by leaving the door ajar while he attended to his shaving and bathing; but his wife insisted that the door should always be shut, and that was that.

One night he decided he must put his fears to the test. So he went along with a lighted candle to have a hot bath — with the door of the room firmly locked from the inside.

Though quite uneasy for no apparent reason at all, he ran hot water from a gas geyser and undressed. As he was testing the heat of the water, a sound in the unlit firegrate made him turn round. But he saw nothing. Thinking it might have been something dropping from the chimney above, he turned his attention once more to his bath. Again, that noise from the grate. But, once more, nothing to indicate the source. After investigating the grate thoroughly, he turned to make for the bath when he slipped and fell on the floor. For some seconds he lay still, recovering his senses and then made to raise himself. Suddenly his candle went out and he found himself in funereal blackness. Quite startled by now, he sensed a rising feeling of terror and his first thought was to get to the door of the bathroom to cry out for more matches for his candle.

Then, quite without warning, there came from the bath the sounds of rubbing and splashing, as though some person was washing vigorously. The water rose and fell, bubbled and gurgled. As if to add to the realism of the sounds, there came gasping and puffing and the soft, smooth sound of a well-soaped flannel.

The next thing to occur was the opening of a cupboard door, slowly and stealthily, and the owner, transfixed in his terror, heard something approach in his direction. Whatever it was came up to him and something touched his naked skin. This was the hemline of silk petticoats, from which exuded the perfume of violets. His terror increased when the ghost of the woman, for such it was, stepped on his chest, placing an icy-cold, high-heeled shoe on him as though he were a doormat. But the ghost was oblivious of his presence. Next, there came the sound of a movement as though the woman had reached the bath, to be followed by violent splashing and gasping. The noises of the bather grew weaker and finally ceased, when the woman turned from the murder which she had obviously committed and made for the fireplace.

The deep blackness in the room was now broken by the sight of the white, luminous face of a woman who was obviously beautiful but whose beauty had turned into something repellent with hate.

Then the face vanished and the owner eventually made for the door of the room, unlocked it, and managed to reach the safety of his bedroom. As with the other times when he had confessed to his wife his uneasiness about the room, she scoffed at his fears and told him to think no more of the matter.

For some days nothing more untoward occurred until one morning when the eldest son in the family was running a bath, he saw, floating in the bath, the body of an old, grey-haired man. It was bloated and had a purple hue; glassy eyes stared at the ceiling. The boy screamed and ran from the room. The household immediately went to the bathroom to investigate the matter, but found nothing in the bath.

The father had remained in the dining room; his own terrifying experience had been sufficient for him. Chiding the boy for his imagination, the family went out into the landing, to come face to face with a handsome woman dressed in costly silks and jewellery. She glided past them with silent footsteps and disappeared into a cupboard.

The reason for the owner's uneasiness was now confirmed. Within a week the house was empty and up for sale. Later inquiries revealed that at one time the house had belonged to a rich old man who had married a beautiful young woman of Spanish descent. The disparity in ages led to quarrels. The man was eventually found dead in his bath; there being no indications of violence, it was generally supposed that he had fainted and accidentally drowned. The young widow, who had inherited all the money, left the house, went abroad and was never seen again.

Still in Glasgow, another house gave the occupant of one of its rooms more than some cause for concern. When the following events occurred, it had been converted into a first-class private hotel, innocent on the outside but containing the essence of something which awaited only the right kind of recipient. The latter eventually turned up, an actor who was playing in Glasgow. For the first three nights in this particular room nothing happened — except that the actor had the most terrifying nightmares, which was unusual for him.

On the fourth night he was awakened by the sound of a loud crash. He sat up and listened for a time, but heard nothing more. Thinking that he had heard the sound in his sleep, he decided that a drink of lime juice from a bottle he kept on the mantelpiece would help to cool his rushing brain. He got up and, in the darkness, made his way to the mantelpiece, first to find matches and then the juice. But try as he might, he could not find the place. Deciding to give up the drink, he groped his way back to the bed, guiding himself by feel round the items of furniture in the room with which he had become familiar. But then he found he could not trace the bed. It was a room of reasonably small dimensions and it seemed to him at first almost a joke that he could lose a bed in such a room. He tried again, but failed. Then, as he stretched his arms in front of him, his fingers came into contact with a noose suspended in mid-air.

Almost as if in a dream, he felt his feet glued to the floor and the noose, with a strange and gentle purring sound, fall about his neck and begin to tighten.

In a mounting feeling of desperation he tried to raise his hands to remove the rope, but found that some power forced them down to his side again. He opened his mouth to cry out, but was unable to utter any sound. Only a cold, icy current of air froze in his lungs. He felt cold, clammy hands tearing his feet from the floor. He was hoisted up and then dropped. A sharp pain shot through his body. He made frantic efforts to release himself, but could not. Then he blacked out. When he recovered he found himself lying on the floor of the room, apparently suffering from nothing else but a chill.

The next night, determined to prevent a recurrence of what he had experienced, he left a candle burning and went to sleep. Later in the night he woke up in darkness. A curious smell attracted his notice. At first he thought he was dreaming, but the smell grew stronger, the pungent odour of drugs or, at the very least, the same strong smell as one meets in an old chemist's shop. As his mind tried to grasp what was happening to him, his face came in contact with something cold and flabby. This caused him to react so violently that he fell out of bed and onto the floor.

The fall convinced him of one thing — that he was not dreaming. Getting up to go into bed again, he froze in his movements. For he saw the bed was occupied. In the middle of the pillow was a face: the face of his brother who at the time was supposed to be living in New York. His brother's appearance was startling: the mouth was open, the tongue was swollen, and the face was a yellow colour tinged with a livid, lurid black. Then the brother spoke: 'I have been wanting to speak to you for ages, but something I cannot explain has always prevented me. I have been dead a month; not cancer, but Dolly. Poison. Good-bye. I shall rest in peace now.'

The voice stopped. There was a rush of cold air, faintly scented with the odour of drugs, and then the face vanished.

The following morning a letter arrived from Dolly, his brother's wife, to say that the brother had died of cancer in the throat.

The experience of a couple who were touring Scotland in the years of the 1880s is particularly interesting in that the spirit manifestation caused terror and physical sickness. The couple arrived in Dundee and were directed to a hotel, previously an inn, near the Perth Road. They were delighted with the place at first sight. Being an old building, it exuded a pleasant atmosphere of old-world charm. The interior was no less pleasing: low ceilings, oak beams, polished wood floors, diamond-lattice windows and numerous nooks and crannies. The hotel was full, however, and the only accommodation the proprietor could offer was a room at the end of a long passage leading to the back of the building. It was a large room, with a big ebony four-poster bed in a recess. A deep and dark cupboard was let into the wall directly facing the bed.

The couple were not at all superstitious, except in so far as they discussed how many memories were associated with such an old building. More than that was not discussed. Yet, when the couple undressed for bed the woman sensed a curious sensation as she rummaged in the cupboard.

Some time after, a nearby church tower bell had struck midnight, the woman woke to become aware of a smell in the room. It was pungent and most offensive. It was so strong that it crept up her nostrils and brought her out in a cold release of perspiration. The smell overpowered her and she decided to trace it, half-knowing in her mind that it could not be other than associated with something horrible and strange. She got up from the bed, taking care not to wake her husband, and traced the source of the smell to the same dark cupboard which had upset her earlier. By the time she reached the cupboard door the stench was almost suffocating. She paused for a few minutes; one voice within her told her to get back to her bed, but the other told her to satisfy her curiosity and open the door.

At last, the latter voice dominated and she opened the door. No sooner had she done so than the room began to fill with a faint phosphorescent glow and she saw opposite her a human head floating in mid-air. It was the head of a man, red-haired and in an advanced state of decay. She was petrified and quite unable to cry out to her husband. Then, as the head began to move towards her, she screamed and fled to the bed, followed by the floating head. Her husband woke up at the sound and was even more terrified than his wife as the head hovered over the bed. He tried to utter a prayer, but not one syllable came from his dry throat.

He managed to stretch out his hand to the floor of the room and grasp his walking stick. With both hands, he brought it down on the head. The result was as they might have expected. The stick met with no resistance and came down on the bedclothes. The head continued its advance towards them. The couple jostled to get out of the bed together, and in their haste both fell on the floor. With the head now hovering over them, they could do nothing but watch it in terror. It descended lower and lower until it passed right through them and through the floor; then it vanished.

The couple took the next few hours until dawn to recover from their experience, and in the morning demanded an explanation from the landlord. At first he was reluctant to offer any explanation, and tried to convince them that it had been a nightmare. But they insisted and were eventually told the story.

' What am I to do? I cannot shut up a house on which I have taken a twenty years' lease, and, after all, there is only one visitor in twenty who is disturbed by the apparition. What is the history of the head? It is said to be that of a pedlar who was murdered here over a hundred years ago. The body was hidden behind the wainscoting, and his head hidden under the cupboard floor. The miscreants were never caught; they are supposed to have gone down in a ship that sailed from this port just about that time and was never heard of again.'

A hotel, now demolished, in Aberdeen was the scene of another mysterious manifestation. On this particular occasion a nurse was called in to look after one of the hotel guests, a Miss Vining. The hotel proprietor knew nothing about his guest except that she had been an actress and was now ill of a disease which was oriental in origin. The nurse was required to be with her patient almost continuously. Her first meeting with Miss Vining was strange. No sooner had she entered the sick room than she became aware of a gloom which seemed to hang over her like a huge shadow. And when she approached the sick woman on her bed, the feeling she received was of something trying to force itself between her and her patient.

The patient being too ill even to converse, the nurse settled down beside the bed for a vigil. Contrary to her expectations, the first night passed without incident. On the second night, however, at about ten o'clock, she had just registered her patient's temperature and had sat down when something caused her to look across to a chair on the other side of the bed. It was occupied by a child, a tiny girl.

Rather startled at the sight, she rose to chide the child for being in the sickroom, and to ask how she entered the room without being noticed. But the child lifted a hand and motioned her back. Unable to help herself, the nurse stood where she was. How long she was almost entranced she did not know. Then, a long-drawn-out sigh from her patient took her attention. Again she made to move but was once more stilled by the raised hand of the child. She sat down, and then, so overcome by her efforts to remove the state of inertia into which the child had placed her, she fell asleep. When she later woke there was no sign of the child. She turned her attention to the patient who was delirious and had a high temperature. Administering her drugs, the temperature was reduced and Miss Vining relaxed until the hours of the morning.

Telling the doctor of the child's visit, the nurse was told that on no account was any person to visit the sick woman and advised her to lock the door of the bedroom. The next night, with the door firmly locked, the nurse settled down to a night's vigil. The long hours passed and she nodded off. A sob from her patient roused her and, looking at the bed, caught sight of the same child again. Once more the nurse rose to chase the child away when, raising her small hand, the child's power virtually paralysed the nurse.

A long time passed as the child sat there watching the sick woman endure another delirious spell, and the nurse sat transfixed, unable to do or say anything. Then, at last, the child rose and moved from the bed towards the window. The nurse found her voice and cried after the child. She reached over and snatched the child's hat. It melted away in her hand and, to her horror, the child's face, previously pretty, now turned into the face of a corpse of a Hindu child with a big, gaping cut in its throat. At that sight the nurse fainted.

When she recovered, all ghostly manifestations were gone. And the patient was dead. One of her hands was thrown across her eyes, as if to shut out some object on which she feared to look, while the other hand grasped the counterpane with a grip of terror.

After the burial, the nurse was asked by the hotel proprietor to pack up Miss Vining's things, among which was found a photograph of a Hindu child dressed in the same clothes as was worn by the ghostly child. On the reverse of the picture were the words: 'Natalie. May God forgive us both.'

Nothing more was ever seen of the child ghost or of the Hindu child. But not long after Miss Vining's death, the hotel became haunted — by the ghost of a woman.

A most unusual story is associated with a house near Ayr. It was a two-storey building, with a main wing and a side construction. It was full of rooms and wandering corridors, leading from the large hall which sported a gallery running round it. This house was haunted by a golden light which had the perfume of heliotropes. On one occasion a visitor to the house, so charmed with the whole building and its casual planning, decided to explore. After spending some time in the main building, a search was begun on the side construction. At the foot of its ivy-covered walls and straight in their centre was a wide bed of white flowers; no flowers of other colours were seen. Though curious at the sight of the garden, the visitor thought it best not to enquire as to the reason for the lack of colour. Some evenings later the visitor made a careful way in the dark towards that side of the house next to the new wing. Arriving at the end of a long corridor, she found herself in the middle of the gallery overlooking the large entrance hall. Making further progress, she was stopped by a cry from near at hand. It was a blood-curdling shriek which began in a low key and climbed up through the spine and into the mind to end in a high-pitched piercing. In a sweat of fear she looked around but saw nothing and the house was silent.

After a few moments she proceeded down the next corridor and eventually came to the side wing. Glancing through the window, to where the garden of white flowers lay, she caught sight of, not white flowers, but golden blooms. Then, as she looked, the garden disappeared and its place was taken by a room. Again, as she took in all the details of the furniture, the large open bay window, and the decoration, a door opened and in walked a young girl, carrying a bunch of heliotrope. Less than a moment later, the girl stepped back. A wild wave of terror distorted her face and the room disappeared to leave the scene a simple garden of white flowers.

The next morning, the visitor mentioned what she had seen and was told of the occasion when, forty years previously, the garden had in fact been a room extension, since taken down and replaced by the garden. One night, the house was broken into by burglars, through the window of the room. A relation of the owners was sleeping in it at the time, and with the noise of the intruders she woke and screamed. In panic and in a fit of desperation, the burglars murdered the girl to silence her. Her haunting, since the tragedy, has since been in the form of a shaft of light followed by a scent of heliotrope.

Glamis Castle has been mentioned elsewhere with regard to its ghostly associations. The castle is of an ancient though uncertain date; it is reckoned to have been in existence at the beginning of the eleventh century. From time to time, extra building has changed the original shape, and interior alterations have taken place, but the traditional associations with the supernatural have hardly changed at all. It is said that in the castle tower

Beast of Glamis

there is a room, hidden in some unexpected quarter, which is known only to three people at any one time. The following story is the experience of a woman who stayed at Glamis Castle late last century.

At her own request, placing no credence in the stories she had heard about the hauntings, she was given a bedroom in the tower. On her first night, before she retired, she had a good supper and then

climbed into bed. Within minutes she was asleep.
Then she woke up — and found herself in an oddly-
shaped room with a high ceiling. The floor was of
blackened oak. A window was set high up in the
wall, quite inaccessible from the floor. The walls
were covered with some kind of drapery. The
furniture seemed to her to be more appropriate to
the cell of a prison or lunatic asylum. There was
no chair; only a coarse deal table, a straw mattress
and a kind of trough. An air of irrepressible gloom
hung about the place, which increased in its inten-
sity as she looked with mounting fear.

For some inexplicable reason she found herself,
not in her bed, but standing in the room with her
eyes fixed on one corner. It was in the shadow and
nothing with any kind of shape was discernible.
Then something moved. The gentle rubbing of a
soft body on the floor, breathing, one or two small
cracking noises and slowly the thing in the corner
began to make itself known. The body was hunched.
The legs were crooked and mis-shapen. The arms
were unduly long, with crooked, knotty fingers. The
head was large and bestial, with hair that fell around
the face in tangled masses. In a slow, lumbering
movement, the shape lunged towards the onlooker.
Before anything else could happen, the handle of the
door turned and another person entered; at the
same time, the whole tower seemed to reverberate
with the most appalling animal screams. Then she
found herself sitting up in bed with the screams
still in her ears only, for the night and her room
were as silent as they had always been.

Another woman had an experience which remained with her for the rest of her life. She, too, was given a room in the tower of Glamis Castle and was a firm sceptic whenever the subject of ghosts cropped up.

On her first night, after a long journey from Edinburgh, she was glad of the comfort of her bed, and fell asleep the moment her head touched the pillow. But not for long. Even through her deep sleep she was startled awake by the sound of a loud noise. She listened for it again, but all was silent. Then, as the minutes fled by, she became aware of an unnatural feeling in the air, as though the silence was a prelude to some coming event. As she listened further, she heard a low, distinct noise, repeated in rapid succession. She realised that the sound was that of mailed footsteps racing up the long flight of stairs at the end of the corridor leading to her room. The sounds drew nearer and grew louder. Almost outside the door of her room there came other noises: the banging and clanking of sword scabbards, the panting and gasping of men, sore pressed and obviously fighting for their lives. Two men in particular were fighting a duel to the death. Through the stout wood of the door, the listener heard every detailed noise made by the men, including, once, when one of the men was hurled back by a tremendous blow which sent him reeling heavily against the door. The blow was repeated and a cry rose in the victim's throat that developed into a gurgling groan.

Immediately there followed the distinct sound of

a body drained of life slithering in heavy armour down against the door; then followed the final clang of metal as the victim fell dead. There was a pause, as though the victor was considering his next move. A movement under the door attracted her attention. Slowly, taking its time, a dark stream of fluid lapped its way into the room. In her dismay the woman screamed aloud. There was a sudden stir from outside the room, and the next moment — despite the fact that the door was securely locked — it slowly opened. The limits of her endurance reached saturation point at that moment and she fainted, to wake up some hours later with a welcome stream of morning sunshine coming in from her window.

With some doubt, she argued that her experience had been the result of extreme exhaustion after the journey from Edinburgh, and chose to sleep in the same room on the following night. After a day spent walking on the moors, she lay down on her bed and dozed off in a light sleep. Suddenly she woke up to find herself face to face with a huge figure in bright armour. The visor was up, and from the opening a face leered at her; a face long since dead, but still with the smile of the living on it. The figure bent lower over her, and before anything further could happen a rap on the door, heralding a maid with some tea, caused the figure to vanish.

A final story about the castle reads more like fiction, but is related as being true in its details. About the middle of last century a man was lodging at a hotel near the Strathmore Estate. Having a deep interest in antiquities, he went into the castle grounds one day. Looking around, he was met by a man whom he took to be a gardener. The man's features were unusual: high cheek-bones, a mass of red hair, and a hawk-like shape to the face. He asked the gardener if he knew of any antique objects found in the grounds of the castle. The latter said that he had something of particular interest, and both men went down a track to a cottage.

The item was in fact the skeleton of a hand, with abnormally large knuckles, and the first joint — of both fingers and thumb — much shorter than the others.

The item was indeed unusual, so much so that the gardener was offered a good price for the relic. But the gardener refused the money, and offered it free, with words of caution that it was not a canny thing to have about one's house.

The caution went unheeded, for the buyer was a hard-headed man from London who paid no attention to the superstitions of Highlanders, who saw fairies as often as they blinked their eyes.

That evening, he studied the skeleton hand by candlelight. It was indeed an unusual specimen for his collection, and he warmed in anticipation of the envious comments his friends would make. Towards midnight he decided to retire and was about to put his things away when he caught sight of the mirror opposite him. In it he saw the door of his room was open. He turned round to close the door, but saw it was already closed. Thinking he had experienced an optical illusion, he looked in the mirror again:

the door was open. Then, as he looked into the mirror more closely he fancied he saw a large black shadow in the doorway. A shiver ran up his spine and for a moment he felt a pang of fear. He turned round — the door was as firmly shut as it had been the last time he looked.

Despite some misgivings, he decided to keep looking in the mirror to see what was about to happen. The darkness in the doorway was there when he looked again, only this time it moved to take the shape of a huge spider or some odd-shaped bird. But the whole was so indistinct that he was unable to say exactly what it was. Slowly the shadow drew near to him and the experience so fascinated him that even if he had been able to, he felt he must remain seated to participate in what he felt sure was about to happen. The next thing he realised was that the shadowy form coming closer to him was forming into a hand — the skeleton of the hand he had got from the gardener at Glamis Castle. This time, however, the hand was covered with mouldering flesh. It moved towards the back of his chair and then he felt its cold and clammy touch on his head. It pressed downwards and almost suffocated him. Yet, all this was happening to him as he looked in the mirror. It was as though his imagination had run riot.

Suddenly he found himself in a room from which all his familiar furniture had disappeared. It was bare and comfortless, strangely constructed, without a door. Only a narrow slit of a window near the ceiling admitted light.

In one corner of the room lay a mattress on which lay a form, huddled up as though in the cold. He found, to his surprise, that he had a knife in his hands and, try as he did, he could not dispel the thoughts of murder that were forming in his mind. With a cold and calculating stealth, he approached the mattress. With his hand raised high, he brought the knife down and plunged it into the side of the form. Then he recrossed the room and found himself in his hotel apartment once more.

His first reaction was to look for the skeleton of the hand. But it was not where he had left it. It had vanished completely. His room door was still shut. A final reaction was to look in the mirror and he saw, not his own face, but that of the gardener leering out of the glass.

The following day, intent on getting some further explanation about the skeleton hand, he went to Glamis Castle and looked for the gardener. Unable to find him, he decided to call in at the cottage, but was unable to find the building. Enquiries revealed that no one knew about the cottage, nor did they know of the gardener. Completely mystified, he returned to London by way of Edinburgh.

Stopping in the capital for a day or so, he took it in his mind to visit a loan exhibition of pictures in one of the city's galleries. As he wandered past the portraits, all thoughts of his terrifying experience gone from his mind, he halted abruptly. Before him was the portrait of a gentleman in an ancient costume, with the face of the gardener of Glamis Castle. The thick red hair, the hawk-like features and leering eyes were those of the character he had met in the grounds of the castle, but who did not exist except, perhaps, in his own time in the past.

Mystery painting

HAUNTED HOUSES

HAUNTED houses abound throughout the Scottish countryside. The house is probably more often associated with ghostly manifestations than more obvious places such as churchyards. Ghosts in no way seem to confine themselves to old buildings, as might again be expected. Comparatively recent dwellings such as Council houses have their fair share of ghostly happenings, unexplained noises and unnerving sights. In more than a few instances of ghostly manifestations in occupied houses the residents have resorted to exorcism to get rid of their unwanted and uninvited guests. Other people accept the supernatural and allow their ghost to wander around. But it all really depends on the ghost (poltergeists are particularly troublesome and tend to make life difficult), and many houses have had to be abandoned to their spirit occupants, attempts at exorcism having been completely futile.

Before Andrew Carnegie, the multi-millionaire, bought Skibo Castle, in Sutherland, the place was said to be haunted. The story relates that the castle was on one occasion left in the sole charge of a

man-servant who had a particularly evil turn of
mind. One night he induced his sweetheart, a local
girl whom he had betrayed, to visit him at the castle.
This the girl agreed to do. But when she failed
to return from her visit, a hue and cry was raised.
Despite an intensive search, she was never found. In
time suspicion fell on the castle servant. The whole
building was subjected to a thorough search. The
fellow protested his innocence; the missing girl was
not found, and the whole affair became a local
mystery. Shortly afterwards the servant left both the
castle and the district and, soon after he had done
so, people living in the castle found themselves to
be regularly startled by unearthly screams in the
corridors and by the sight of the ghost of a young
woman who appeared always to be in great terror.
Many years passed until some repairs were required
in the castle buildings, during which a woman's
bones were found in the very spot at which the
apparition usually disappeared. The remains were
buried elsewhere, since when the castle ceased to
be haunted.

Another house in Sutherland had to be abandoned
because of a weird vision which regularly appeared
before the tenants and terrified them so greatly that
they had to flee for their sanity. One local ex-soldier,
brave and fearless in the field of battle and as brave
before the unknown, offered to spend a night in the
house. This he did, and when the ghost eventually
appeared ·he, despite heartbeats thudding against
his chest, asked it the reason for its visits. It replied
that its body had been buried beneath the floor of

the house and if it were to be decently interred in the churchyard it would cease to haunt the house. The following day a search was made and the bones were duly found, buried in the churchyard as requested, and the house became habitable again.

One house in Ross-shire was haunted by a series of inexplicable noises and voices. These a local man decided to investigate and undertook to sleep in the place alone. Shortly before midnight he was awakened by the sound of rats scurrying about in an adjoining room. He thumped a chair beside his bed and the noises stopped. Less than an hour later he was again wakened, this time by a sound as if a hard broom were sweeping the floor in the next room in a very noisy fashion. This time he decided he would investigate and rose to light his lamp. Before he could strike a match he heard a voice in Gaelic plead: 'Let me in, let me in.'

He struck his match, and as soon as he had done so the voice stopped. He listened carefully for some time, but all was silent in the house. He fell asleep again, and for a third time his slumber was disturbed by the rattling of the bedroom door and a feeble voice saying: 'I cannot harm you, but leave this place soon, do, do.'

There was such a degree of substance and reality in the voice that he decided the best course of action was to get a neighbour along to help him search the place, being now convinced that a human agency was behind his experiences. So he dressed and went along to the next house. But the neighbour refused to go along with him. However, he did compensate his unwillingness by telling the story of the house which had been built on the site of an older thatched dwelling from which a poor widow had been forcibly evicted. Before she left she had cursed the new house and all who would ever live in it. While the new house was being built, mysterious lights were often seen flickering about in the uncompleted building. Workmen's tools were found scattered about on several occasions; one of the tenants had become bankrupt and died after a short illness; and another tenant had committed suicide. Eventually the tenants had to leave the place, so unnerved did they become at the ghostly manifestations. Later, as it was a good-built house, other tenants took over and that family were quite happy in it and were never at any time disturbed by any inexplicable and hair-raising noises.

One rather malevolent ghost is that of ' Terrible William,' otherwise Lord Soulis, who is said to haunt Hermitage Castle in Roxburghshire. He had the reputation of being a skilful practitioner of the black arts. Local tradition has it that to get the best out of his magical rites, he would kidnap local children, imprison them in the castle's dungeons, and keep them until he was ready to use them in his foul rites, murdering them and using their blood to make his magic more effective. When eventually news of his deeds became known, the people of the nearby village stormed the building, took him prisoner, bound him in chains, and threw him into a cauldron of boiling lead. After this execution of rough justice, his ghost was seen in and around the castle reenacting the deeds of his erstwhile bad life. In his lifetime he was supposed to have made a pact with Satan who appeared in front of him wearing a cap stained red with the blood of his victims. In exchange for his soul, Lord Soulis was rewarded with the right to summon the Devil by rapping three times on an iron chest.

Summoning Satan

Fyvie Castle, in Aberdeenshire, has a ghost room, a murder room, and a secret room. The famous 'Green Lady' ghost was seen in 1920 wandering about the castle's corridors and disappearing through the panels of a dark wainscotted apartment. A few years before, when a great ugly mass of fungus had appeared in the gun-room, workers discovered a complete skeleton. It was after these bones were removed that disturbances were experienced in the castle. They ceased only when the owner, Lord Beith, requested that the skeleton be rebuilt into the wall again.

Crathes Castle also has its haunted room. A woman, yet another 'Green Lady,' is frequently seen to cross the room and make for an unusually fine carved timber fireplace. When she reaches this spot she is seen to lift a ghostly baby from the hearth. A number of years ago, when workmen were effecting repairs and alterations in the building, the bones of a woman and child were found beneath this fireplace.

Leith Hall, near Kennethmont, Aberdeenshire, is an old family house with a charm of its own. The original nucleus was built about 1650: a rectangular tower house with twin turrets at each of the gables, erected by James Leith. The vicissitudes of the Leith and the Leith-Hay families have filled the house and its grounds with romantic features. The name Hay was added to that of Leith in 1789, on the death of Andrew Hay of Rannes, a Jacobite and pardoned 'rebel' whose lands were inherited by the Leiths. In the grounds is the Dule Tree, from which malefactors were hanged in the days of heritable jurisdiction. The house, perhaps inevitably, has some interesting ghost associations.

Elizabeth Byrd, the author, has recounted many of her experiences while living in Leith Hall in her book, *A Strange and Seeing Time*. Ghostly noises

The Dule Tree — Leith Hall

have been heard (a pibroch of pipe music with counterpoint of drums, and a chanted Mass); ghost smells have been experienced: of food and camphor; sounds, such as heavy footsteps on the third floor and doors closing; and, of course, visual images. The ghost of a woman has been seen in the Historic Wing of the house. Loud, angry voices have been heard on occasions. Miss Byrd's husband, Barrie Gaunt, has related his experience in the haunted master bedroom. He had gone to bed early, but woke about midnight to have a glass of water and enjoy a cigarette. About five minutes after he had put out the light and turned over to go to sleep, he felt — *knew,* he confesses — that someone was moving towards him through the darkness. He relates that he was literally paralysed with horror; for the thing that came towards him was malignant. " Ghosts are not supposed to attack one physically, but I felt that such an attack was imminent." Mr Gaunt found that, try as he might, he could not move. " It was a sort of muscular paralysis. Nor could I seem to catch my breath. I've never felt that sort of fear before . . . About two terrible minutes went by. Then, with my eyes closed so as not to see it, I was able to lunge cross the bed, fumble for the light and turn it on. There was nothing visible."

This kind of experience is common to those who for some reason are unable to ' see ' visual images, but are only too aware of their ability to sense some kind of presence, particularly when it has a malignant character. The writer has had this kind of unpleasant experience and can vouch for the sense of terror it brings and the almost superhuman effort that is required not to succumb to an overwhelming desire to ' go under ' in a swoon of complete and dark oblivion, which may well be the intention of the visiting spirit.

Elizabeth Byrd has recorded that she spent two years alone in that same bedroom, but only towards the end of that period did she sense a feeling of uneasiness before she saw the ghost.

Alanna Knight, the Aberdeen author, has also had paranormal experiences in Leith Hall, and particularly in the nursery where she had a series of " waking dreams " in which she identified with a child accompanied by a governess.

One last, but by no means least, anecdote about Leith Hall, this time from Donella Gordon, of Elgin, who once worked at the hall, in 1929: "The Hon. Lady allowed us to have in our boy friends one night a week. I will never forget, a young couple went along for a quiet spell to the Gun Room, that is under the Music Room. The rest of us were preparing to have our tea and the cakes when along came this young couple. His face was deathly white and his hair standing on end. The girl was sick with fear. They said someone had walked from the Music Room to the Leith bedroom above them *in chains,* moaning and groaning. I know that when we maids had duties in the Leith bedroom we always felt that someone or something would step out of the shadows." It was in this bedroom that Mr Gaunt saw the ghost of a Victorian 'nanny' in broad daylight, surrounded by tourist sightseers.

About three miles from Dingwall, Easter Ross, stands the house of Mountgerald, said to be haunted by the ghost of a workman who was killed during its construction and buried beneath the foundations as a sacrifice. His ghost has been seen on a number of occasions around the spot where he was killed (a large block of stone fell on him) in a large cellar at the bottom of the stairs leading to the basement. To this spot the ghost of the unfortunate man is bound for all time except for five nights in each year: at New Year, Midsummer, the Spring and Autumn Solstices, and on the anniversary of his death, which occurs in the middle of the month of August. As he had been in life a disliked and vindictive kind of person, so he is in death, and he is said to be capable of wreaking his vengeance on anyone sleeping in the house on his ' free ' nights. One friend of previous tenants of Montgerald died on the evening of the August anniversary, who had otherwise been in good health.

The Doune of Rothiemurchus, Inverness-shire, has a ghost and a haunted room, according to local tradition and ken.

A curious story was once in common circulation in the Isle of Harris, Outer Hebrides. This concerned the ' Coffee House ' at Leverburgh. Many years ago, about the 1850s, a building was erected by the Countess of Dunmore, the proprietrix of Harris, for the purpose of providing fishermen with a place for meals, and to offer some suitable accommodation to casual travellers in the islands. For many years, the house proved to be a popular meeting place, both for local people and visitors on both business and pleasure. The story of the Coffee House has its origins just after the turn of this century when many strange knocking sounds began to be heard and cause no end of disturbance to the occupants. The noises, it was noticed, were particularly confined to an area in the region of a bedroom which was occupied by some maids working in the house. The knocking noises often became so unbearable that there was talk of abandoning the building; indeed, the point was eventually reached where the occupants became afraid to sleep in the house alone.

Several weeks after these noises began, the maids

were transferred to a room in another part of the house. But the knocking followed them to their new room. Just when the owners became desperate with despair, one of the maids approached the mistress of the house and said that she was leaving her employ. Thinking that the reason for the girl's sudden decision was the noises, the girl said: 'The knocking has nothing to do with you. It follows me wherever I go.' And, indeed, the knocking stopped on the day this maid left Leverburgh. Afterwards there were no further disturbances experienced in the house. A couple of years later the Coffee House was destroyed by fire. But its ruins were regarded by the local people as being still haunted for a long time after the disaster.

Coffee House Fire